EVERYDAY SPANISH

by Sue Finnie and Danièle Bourdais

translated by Libby Mitchell

Copyright © **ticktock Entertainment Ltd** 2008
First published in Great Britain in 2008 by **ticktock Media Ltd**,
2 Orchard Business Centre, North Farm Road, Tunbridge Wells, Kent, TN2 3XF

written by Sue Finnie and Danièle Bourdais
Spanish translation by Libby Mitchell
ticktock project editor: Joe Harris
ticktock project designer: Simon Fenn
ticktock picture researcher: Lizzie Knowles
Spanish language consultant: Iñaki Alegre

ISBN-13: 978 1 84696 783 2 pbk

Printed in China

Picture credits (t=top; b=bottom; c=centre; l=left; r=right):
age fotostock/ SuperStock: 25t. BananaStock/ SuperStock: 10tr, 11tc, 16tl, 16tr, 21tl. Corbis/
SuperStock: 10tl. Creatas/ SuperStock: 23tl. ImageSource/ SuperStock: 8tr, 12t. iStock: OFC, 1, 5b,
6tc, 7bl, 8bl, 9tl, 11c x2, 13t (sister), 13c (uncle), 13b (snake), 15tr, 15cr, 15bl, 15fbc, 16cr, 16bl, 19tc,
19tr, 20tl, 20c (coffee), 20bl (hotel), 22c (dress), 24cr, 27tl, 27tr, 28tl, 28cl, 29tl, 29cl, 29cc, 29bl,
29bc, 30tl, 30cl, 30cr, 31tl, 31tc, 31cr, 31bc x2, OBCb. Jupiter Images: 12b, 14b, 18tl, 26tl, 29br.
Photo alto/ SuperStock: 31cr. Photodisc/ SuperStock: 7br. Photolibrary Group: 26tr. Purestock/
SuperStock: 7tr, 24tl. Shutterstock: 2, 4 all, 5c, 6tl, 6tr x2, 6b all, 7tl, 7tc, 7c all, 8b (clocks), 9b all, 10b
all, 11tl, 11tr, 11cl, 11cr, 11b all, 12c, 13 all, 14t, 14cl, 14cr, 15tl, 15tc x2, 15cl, 15cc x2, 15bc x2,
15br, 15fbl, 15fbc, 15fbr, 16cl, 16br, 17 all, 18tr, 18c all, 18b all, 19b all, 20tr, 20b all, 21tr, 21b all,
22 all, 23tr, 23b all, 24tr, 24cl, 24c, 24b all, 25cl, 25cr, 25b all, 26b all, 27bl, 27br, 28tc, 28tr, 28cc,
28bl, 28bc x2, 28br, 29tc, 29tr, 29cr, 30tc, 30tr, 30cc, 30bl, 31tr, 31cc, 31bl, 31br x2, 32cr, OBCt.
ticktock Media archive: 5t. Neil Tingle/ actionplus: 19tl. David Young-Wolff/ Alamy: 8tl.

Every effort has been made to trace copyright holders, and we apologise in advance for any omissions.
We would be pleased to insert the appropriate acknowledgments in any subsequent
edition of this publication.

CONTENTS

GETTING STARTED

400 million people all over the world speak Spanish. Why not join them?

In this book, you'll learn 500 essential words and phrases so you can communicate in all kinds of everyday situations, from making friends to shopping for clothes or finding your way round!

Each Spanish word comes with its English translation and an indication of how to pronounce it. Capitals show where the stress falls in a word.

un ordenador . . . . Spanish word
oon or-den-a-DOR . . . . . . *rough pronunciation*
a computer . . . . English translation

For more tips on how to pronounce Spanish words, check out the pronunciation guide on page 32.

Here are just some of the countries where Spanish is spoken:

España
es-PAN-ya
Spain

Colombia
co-LOM-bee-a
Colombia

Costa Rica
COS-ta REE-ka
Costa Rica

México
MEH-hi-co
Mexico

Chile
CHI-leh
Chile

Panamá
pan-a-MA
Panama

Argentina
ar-hen-TEE-na
Argentina

Cuba
COO-ba
Cuba

Venezuela
be-ne-THWE-la
Venezuela

Perú
PEH-roo
Peru

SPAIN FACTS

- 45 million people live in Spain.

- The Spanish flag is yellow and red.

- The capital of Spain is Madrid.

- Spanish money is the euro.

- Spain is the second most mountainous country in Europe, after Switzerland.

- Be careful when crossing the road in Spain! The Spanish drive on the right.

UK
◆ London

Madrid
◆
Spain

KEY WORDS

Quizás.
Key-THAS.
Maybe.

Claro!
CLAR-o!
Of course!

Sí.
See.
Yes.

No.
No.
No.

No sé.
No seh.
I don't know.

Perdón.
Per-DON.
Sorry.

HELP!

If you don't understand what a Spanish person is saying to you, here are some useful phrases:

¿Puede repetirlo, por favor?
PWEH-deh reh-peh-TEER-lo, por fa-BOR?
Could you repeat that, please?

No entiendo.
No en-tee-YEN-do.
I don't understand.

¿Habla inglés?
HAB-la ing-LES?
Do you speak English?

¿Cómo se dice...?
CO-mo seh DEE-theh?
How do you say...?

Sometimes the Spanish word that you use will depend on whether you are male or female.

This symbol (♀) shows that a word describes a woman or girl.

This (♂) shows that a word describes a man or boy.

MAKING NEW FRIENDS

¿Cómo te llamas?
CO-mo teh YA-mas?
What's your name?

Me llamo Anna.
Meh YA-mo An-a.
My name's Anna.

¡Hola!
O-la!
Hello!

¿Qué tal?
Keh tal?
How are you?

¿Qué idiomas hablas?
Keh i-dee-O-mas AB-las?
What languages do you speak?

Hablo inglés y español.
HAB-lo ing-GLES ee es-pan-YOL.
I speak English and Spanish.

¿De dónde eres?
Deh DON-deh EH-res?
Where are you from?

Soy del Reino Unido.
Soy del RAY-no oo-NEE-do.
I'm from Britain.

España
es-PAN-ya
Spain

Italia
ee-TA-lee-a
Italy

Polonia
po-LON-ee-a
Poland

Francia
FRAN-thee-a
France

Alemania
al-eh-MAN-ee-a
Germany

China
CHEE-na
China

Tengo novio.♂/
Tengo novia.♀
TEN-go NO-bee-o./
TEN-go NO-bee-a.
I have a boyfriend/
a girlfriend.

¿Me das tu número
de móvil?
Meh das too NOO-meh-ro
deh MO-beel?
Can you give me your
mobile number?

¿Quieres bailar conmigo?
Kee-AIR-es by-LAR con-MEE-go?
Do you want to dance with me?

¿Qué te gusta?
Keh teh GOOS-ta?
What are you into?

la moda
la MO-da
fashion

bailar
by-LAR
dancing

el deporte
el de-POR-teh
sport

las películas
las peh-LEE-coo-las
films

los videojuegos
los bee-deh-o-
HWEH-goss
video games

¿Me das tu email?
Meh das too e-MAIL?
Can you give me your email
address?

Mi dirección de email es...
Mee dee-rec-thee-ON deh
e-MAIL es...
My email is...

¡Adiós!
A-dee-OS!
Good bye!

¡Hasta luego!
AS-ta LWEH-go!
See you soon!

IT'S A DATE

¿Cuántos años tienes?
QUAN-tos AN-yos tee-EH-nes?
How old are you?

Tengo quinze años.
TENG-go KEEN-theh AÑ-yos.
I'm fifteen years old.

¿Cuándo es tu cumpleaños?
QUAN-do es too cum-pleh-AN-yos?
When's your birthday?

Mi cumpleaños es el once de mayo.
Mee cum-pleh-AN-yos es el ON-theh deh MY-yo.
My birthday's on the 11th of May.

¿Cuántos?
QUAN-tos?
How many?

1	2	3	4	5	6	7	8	9	10	11
uno	dos	tres	cuatro	cinco	seis	siete	ocho	nueve	diez	once
OO-no	*dos*	*tres*	*QUA-tro*	*THEEN-co*	*SAY-is*	*see-YET-eh*	*O-cho*	*NWAY-beh*	*dee-ETH*	*ON-theh*
one	two	three	four	five	six	seven	eight	nine	ten	eleven

12	13	14	15	16	17	18	19	20
doce	trece	catorce	quinze	dieciséis	diecisiete	dieciocho	diecinueve	veinte
DO-theh	*TRE-theh*	*ka-TOR-theh*	*KIN-theh*	*dee-eth-ee-SEH-is*	*dee-eth-ee-see-YE-tay*	*dee-eth-ee-OCH-o*	*dee-eth-ee-NWEH-beh*	*BAIN-teh*
twelve	thirteen	fourteen	fifteen	sixteen	seventeen	eighteen	nineteen	twenty

¿Qué hora es?
Kay OR-a es?
What's the time?

las seis y cuarto
las SAY-is ee QUAR-toh
quarter past six

las cuatro y diez
las QUA-tro ee dee-ETH
ten past four

las diez y media
las dee-ETH ee MED-ee-a
half past ten

las dos menos veinte
las dos MEN-os VAIN-teh
twenty to two

las doce menos cuarto
las DO-theh MEN-os QUAR-toh
quarter to twelve

la una
la OO-na
one o'clock

Los días de la semana
Los DEE-as deh la se-MA-na
Days of the week

El viernes por la tarde a las siete.
El bee-AIR-nes por la TAR-deh a las see-YET-eh.
See you at seven o'clock on Friday evening.

martes
MAR-tes
Tuesday

miércoles
mi-AIR-col-es
Wednesday

lunes
LOO-nes
Monday

jueves
HWEH-bes
Thursday

domingo
do-MIN-go
Sunday

viernes
bee-AIR-nes
Friday

sábado
SA-bad-o
Saturday

El año
El AN-yo
The year

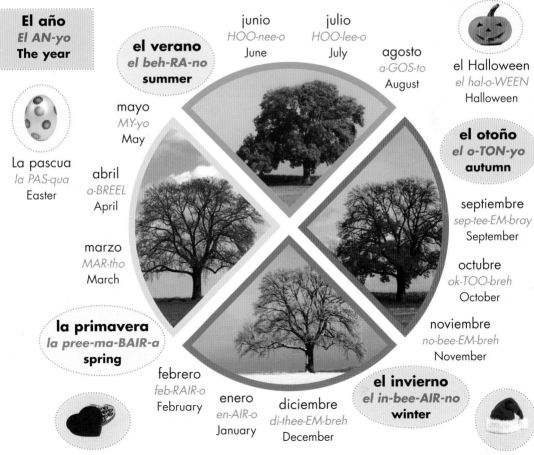

el verano
el beh-RA-no
summer

junio
HOO-nee-o
June

julio
HOO-lee-o
July

agosto
a-GOS-to
August

el Halloween
el hal-o-WEEN
Halloween

mayo
MY-yo
May

el otoño
el o-TON-yo
autumn

La pascua
la PAS-qua
Easter

abril
a-BREEL
April

septiembre
sep-tee-EM-bray
September

octubre
ok-TOO-breh
October

marzo
MAR-tho
March

noviembre
no-bee-EM-breh
November

la primavera
la pree-ma-BAIR-a
spring

febrero
feb-RAIR-o
February

enero
en-AIR-o
January

diciembre
di-thee-EM-breh
December

el invierno
el in-bee-AIR-no
winter

el Día de San Valentín
el DEE-a deh san ba-len-TEEN
Valentine's Day

La Navidad
La na-bee-DATH
Christmas

SNACK ATTACK!

¿Qué quiere?
Keh kee-EH-reh?
What would you like?

¡Mi comida preferida es una hamburguesa y un batido!
Mee co-MEE-da pref-eh-REE-da es OO-na am-burg-WEH-sa ee oon bat-EE-do!
My favourite meal is hamburger and milkshake!

El menú
El me-NOO
Menu

el pollo
el POL-yo
chicken

las pastas
las PAS-tas
pasta

el pan
el pan
bread

el jamón
el ha-MON
ham

el sándwich
el SAND-wich
a sandwich

las verduras
las bair-DOO-ras
green vegetables

las patatas fritas
las pa-TA-tas FREE-tas
chips

la ensalada mixta
la en-sa-LA-da MIX-ta
mixed salad

la pizza
la PEET-za
pizza

la sopa
la SO-pa
soup

Bebo leche por la mañana.
BEH-bo LE-cheh por la man-YA-na.
I drink milk in the morning.

Como ensalada todos los días.
CO-mo en-sa-LA-da TO-dos los DEE-as.
I eat salad every day.

Odio la fruta!
O-dee-o la FROO-ta!
I hate fruit!

De beber
Deh beh-BER
Drinks

un zumo de naranja
oon THOO-mo deh na-RAN-ha
an orange juice

un vaso de agua
oon BA-so deh A-gwa
a glass of water

un chocolate caliente
oon cho-co-LA-teh cal-ee-EN-teh
a hot chocolate

un refresco
oon re-FRES-co
a fizzy drink

Los helados
Los eh-LA-dos
Ice cream

¿Qué sabores tiene?
Keh sa-BOR-es tee-EN-neh?
What flavours have you got?

café
KA-feh
coffee

vainilla
By-NEE-ya
vanilla

fresa
FREH-sa
strawberry

chocolate
cho-ko-LA-teh
chocolate

limón
lee-MON
lemon

menta
MEN-ta
mint

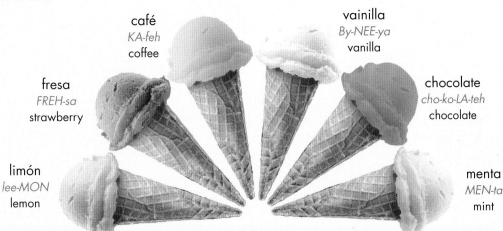

WHO'S WHO?

1 Tiene el pelo rubio.
Tee-EN-neh el PEH-lo ROO-bee-oh.
She's got blonde hair.

2 las orejas con agujero
las o-REH-has con a-goo-HAIR-oh
pierced ears

3 el pelo largo
el PEH-lo LAR-go
long hair

4 Los ojos azules
los O-hos a-THOOL-es
blue eyes

5 el pelo liso
el PEH-lo LEE-so
straight hair

6 las gafas
las GA-fas
glasses

7 un flequillo
oon fle-KIL-yo
a fringe

8 la boca
la BO-ka
mouth

9 los dientes
los dee-EN-tes
teeth

10 un aparato dental
oon a-pa-RA-to den-TAL
braces

11 la nariz
la na-REETH
nose

12 Tiene el pelo negro.
Tee-EN-neh el PEH-lo NEH-gro.
He's got black hair.

13 el pelo corto
el PEH-low COR-to
short hair

14 los ojos marrones
los O-hos ma-RON-es
brown eyes

15 la mejilla
la meh-HEEL-ya
cheek

16 la barbilla
la bar-BEE-ya
chin

17 el cuello
el QUEL-yo
neck

Ésta es mi familia.
ES-ta es mee fa-MEEL-i-a.
Here's my family.

¿Tienes hermanos?
Tee-EN-es air-MA-nos?
Have you got any brothers and sisters?

Tengo dos hermanos y una hermana.
Ten-go dos air-MA-nos ee OO-na air-MA-na
I've got two brothers and a sister.

mi padre
mee PA-dreh
my dad

mi madre
mee MA-dreh
my mum

mi hermano
mee air-MA-no
my brother

mi hermana
mee air-MA-na
my sister

YO
yo
me

mi abuela
mee a-BWE-la
my grandmother

mi abuelo
mee a-BWE-lo
my grandfather

mi primo
mee PREE-mo
my cousin

mi tía
mee TEE-a
my aunt

mi tío
mee TEE-o
my uncle

Las mascotas
Las mas-CO-tas
Pets

¿Tienes una mascota?
Tee-EN-es OO-na mas-CO-ta?
Have you got any pets?

Tengo un perro.
TEN-go oon PAIR-ro.
I've got a dog.

un ratón
oon ra-TON
a mouse

un hámster
oon AM-stair
a hamster

un periquito
oon peh-ree-KEE-to
a budgie

un gato
oon GA-to
a cat

un pez dorado
oon peth dor-A-do
a goldfish

un conejo
oon con-EH-ho
a rabbit

una serpiente
OO-na sair-pee-EN-teh
a snake

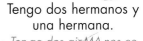

DRESS TO IMPRESS

Prefiero llevar vaqueros y
una camiseta.
*Pre-fee-AIR-o yeh-BAR ba-KEH-ros ee
OO-na cam-ee-SEH-ta.*
My favourite clothes are jeans and t-shirts.

¿Me lo puedo probar?
Meh lo PWEH-do pro-BAR?
Can I try this on?

¿Me queda bien?
Meh KEH-da bee-EN?
Does it suit me?

¡Sí, te queda fenomenal!
See, teh KEH-da fe-no-men-AL!
Yes, it looks great!

Llevo zapatillas deportivas los fines de semana.
*YE-bo tha-pa-TEE-yas deh-por-TEE-bas
los FEE-nes deh se-MA-na.*
I wear trainers at the weekend.

azul	verde	amarillo	naranja	rojo	rosa	violeta	negro	blanco
a-THOOL	*BAIR-deh*	*a-ma-REEL-yo*	*na-RAN-ha*	*RO-ho*	*RO-sa*	*bee-o-LEH-ta*	*NEH-gro*	*BLAN-co*
blue	green	yellow	orange	red	pink	purple	black	white

los pendientes
los pen-dee-EN-tes
earrings

una falda
OO-na FAL-da
a skirt

una gorra
OO-na GOR-a
a cap

una sudadera con
capucha
*OO-na soo-da-DAIR-ra
con ca-POO-cha*
a hooded top

una bufanda
OO-na boo-FAN-da
a scarf

gafas de sol
GA-fas deh sol
sunglasses

una chaqueta
OO-na cha-KEH-ta
a jacket

guantes
GWAN-tes
gloves

un vestido
oon ves-TEE-do
a dress

un bolso
oon BOL-so
a bag

un cinturón
oon thin-too-RON
a belt

pantalones cortos
pan-ta-LO-nes COR-tos
shorts

unas sandalias
OO-nas san-DA-lee-ass
sandals

un jersey
oon her-SEH
a pullover

pantalones
pan-ta-LO-nes
trousers

zapatos
tha-PA-tos
shoes

HI-TECH

Voy a mandarte un mensaje.
Boy a man-DAR-teh oon men-SA-heh.
I'll send a text message.

Hablo con mis amigos por Internet.
AB-lo con mees a-MEE-gos por in-tair-NET.
I chat with my friends on the Internet.

¡Vamos a sacar una foto!
BA-mos a sak-AR OO-na FO-to!
Let's take a photo!

Tengo que mirar mis emails.
TEN-go keh mee-RAR mees e-MAILS.
I need to check my emails.

¡No te olvides de recargar tu móvil!
No teh ol-BEE-des deh reh-car-GAR too MO-beel!
Don't forget to charge your mobile!

Nos gustan los videojuegos.
Nos GOO-stan los bee-day-oh-HWEH-goss.
We love video games.

la radio
la RA-dee-o
radio

una cámara de vídeo
OO-na KA-ma-ra deh BEE-deh-o
camcorder

un (ordenador) portátil
oon (or-den-a-DOR) por-TA-teel
laptop

Un ordenador
Oon or-den-a-DOR
A computer

la pantalla
la pan-TIE-ya
computer screen

la webcam
la web-kam
webcam

el teclado
el te-KLA-do
computer keyboard

un ratón
oon ra-TON
mouse

una cámara
OO-na CA-ma-ra
camera

una consola
OO-na kon-SO-la
games console

un ipod/un mp3
oon ee-pod/oon eh-meh-peh-tres
ipod/mp3 player

una máquina DVD
OO-na MA-kee-na deh-oo-beh-DEH
DVD player

un (teléfono) móvil
oon (teh-LEH-fo-no) MO-beel
mobile phone

un DVD
oon deh-oo-beh-DEH
DVD

la televisión
la tel-eh-bee-see-ON
television

FREE TIME

Toco en una banda.
TO-co en OO-na BAN-da.
I play in a band.

Me gusta el hip-hop.
Meh GOO-sta el hip-hop.
I like hip-hop.

el heavy metal
el HEH-bee MEH-tal
heavy metal

la música pop
la MOO-see-ka pop
pop music

la música de baile
la MOO-see-ka deh BY-leh
dance music

¿Tocas algún instrumento musical?
TO-cas al-GOON ins-troo-MEN-to moo-si-CAL?
Do you play an instrument?

el teclado
el tek-LA-do
keyboard

el piano
el pee-A-no
piano

el violín
el bee-o-LIN
violin

la batería
la bat-air-REE-ya
drums

la guitarra eléctrica
la gee-TAR-ra el-EK-tree-ka
electric guitar

el saxofón
el sax-o-FON
saxophone

la flauta
la FLAU-ta
flute

¿Qué equipo de fútbol
te gusta?
*Keh eh-KEE-po deh
FOOT-bol teh GOO-sta?*
Which football team do
you support?

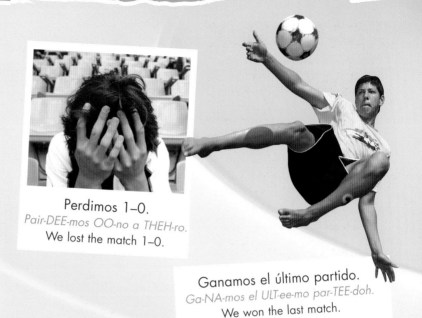

Perdimos 1–0.
Pair-DEE-mos OO-no a THEH-ro.
We lost the match 1–0.

Ganamos el último partido.
Ga-NA-mos el ULT-ee-mo par-TEE-doh.
We won the last match.

¿Qué deportes te gustan?
Keh deh-POR-tes teh GOO-stan?
What sport do you like?

el rugby
el RUG-bee
rugby

el tenis
el TEN-ees
tennis

la equitación
la e-kee-ta-thee-ON
horse-riding

la natación
la na-ta-thee-ON
swimming

el ciclismo
el thee-KLEES-mo
cycling

el atletismo
el at-leh-TEES-mo
running

el yudo
el YOO-do
judo

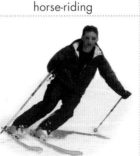

el esquí
el es-KEE
skiing

la escalada
la es-ka-LA-da
rock climbing

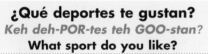

ON THE TOWN

Esta es mi casa.
ES-ta es mee CA-sa.
This is my house.

Vivo en un bloque de pisos.
BEE-bo en oon BLO-keh deh PEE-sos.
I live in a block of flats.

un zoo
oon tho
zoo

un café de Internet
oon ca-FEH deh in-tair-NET
Internet café

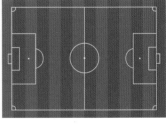

un campo de fútbol
oon CAM-po deh FOOT-bol
football pitch

un centro deportivo
oon THEN-tro de-por-TEE-bo
sports centre

una piscina
OO-na pis-THEE-na
swimming pool

una biblioteca
OO-na bee-blee-o-TEH-ka
library

un hotel
oon o-TEL
hotel

un restaurante
oon res-tau-RAN-teh
a restaurant

una peluquería
OO-na peh-loo-keh-REE-a
hairdresser's

¿Hay un café cerca de aquí?
Ay oon ka-FEH ther-ka day a-KEE?
Is there a coffee shop near here?

¡El parque temático es genial!
El PAR-keh teh-MA-ti-ko es hen-ee-AL!
The theme park is brilliant!

una comisaría de policía
*00-na co-mee-sa-REE-a
deh po-lee-THEE-a*
police station

un museo
oon moo-SEH-oh
museum

correos
co-REH-os
post office

un parque
oon PAR-kay
park

el cine
oon THEE-neh
cinema

un camping
oon KAM-ping
campsite

servicios
sair-BEE-thee-os
toilets

una oficina de turismo
*00-na o-fi-THEE-na deh
too-REES-mo*
tourist information office

un hospital
oon os-pee-TAL
hospital

SHOP TILL YOU DROP

¡Me encanta ir de compras con mis amigos!
Meh en-CAN-ta eer deh COM-pras con mees a-MEE-gos!
I love shopping with my friends!

¿Cuánto es?
QUAN-to es?
How much does this cost?

Veinte euros, por favor.
BAIN-teh EH-oo-ros por fa-BOR.
Twenty euros, please.

una tienda de discos
OO-na tee-EN-da deh DEES-cos
a music shop

una tienda de juegos
OO-na tee-EN-da deh HWEH-gos
a game store

una tienda de ropa
OO-na tee-EN-da deh RO-pa
a clothes shop

una tienda de recuerdos
OO-na tee-EN-da deh re-KWER-dos
a gift shop

una tienda de deportes
OO-na tee-EN-da deh deh-POR-tes
a sports shop

una patelería
OO-na pas-tel-air-EE-a
a cake shop

una zapatería
OO-na tha-pa-tair-EE-a
a shoe shop

un supermercado
oon soo-pair-mair-KA-do
a supermarket

Quisiera dos tarjetas postales, por favor.
Kee-see-AIR-a dos tar-HET-as pos-TAL-es, por fa-VOR.
I'd like two postcards, please.

¡Ay no! Es demasiado caro.
Ay no! Es deh-ma-see-A-do CAR-o.
Oh no! It's too expensive!

un CD
oon theh-DEH
a CD

sellos
SEL-yos
stamps

un paraguas
oon pa-RAG-wass
an umbrella

pilas
PEE-las
batteries

caramelos
ca-ra-MEH-los
sweets

brillo de labios
BREEL-yo deh LAB-ee-os
lip gloss

una revista
OO-na reh-BEE-sta
a magazine

un perfume
oon pair-FOO-meh
perfume

abierto
a-bee-AIR-to
open

cerrado
thair-A-do
closed

ENTRADA

entrada
en-TRA-da
entrance

salida
sa-LEE-da
exit

SCHOOL DAZE

Voy muy bien en matemáticas.
Boy mwee bee-EN en ma-te-MAT-ee-kas.
I'm very good at maths.

El arte no es lo mío.
El ART-eh no es lo MEE-oh.
I'm terrible at art.

¡Tengo mucha tarea!
TEN-go MOO-cha TAR-eh-a!
I have a lot of homework!

Voy al colegio a pie.
Boy al co-LEH-hee-o a pee-EH.
I walk to school.

Voy en autobús.
Boy en au-to-BOOS.
I take the bus.

Las asignaturas
Las a-seec-na-TOO-ras
School subjects

el francés
el fran-THES
French

el español
el es-pan-YOL
Spanish

la geografía
la heh-og-ra-FEE-a
Geography

la historia
la his-TOR-ee-a
History

las ciencias
las thee-EN-thee-as
Science

la informática
la in-for-MAT-ee-ka
I.C.T.

el teatro
el teh-A-tro
Drama

la tecnología
la tek-no-lo-HEE-a
Technology

la educación
física
la e-du-ka-thee-ON
FEE-si-ka
P.E.

En el aula
En el OW-la
Inside the classroom

el profe
el PRO-feh
teacher

una pizarra
OO-na pee-THA-ra
a board

los alumnos
los a-LUM-nos
students

un pupitre
oon poo-PEE-treh
a desk

una silla
OO-na SEEL-ya
a chair

Las clases empiezan
a las nueve
menos cuarto.
*Las CLA-ses em-pee-EH-than
a las NWEH-beh MEH-nos
QUAR-to.*
School starts at 8:45.

Las clases terminan a
las tres y media.
*Las CLA-ses
tair-MEE-nan a las
tres ee MEH-dee-a.*
School finishes at 3:30.

En la mochila
En la mo-CHEE-la
In my school bag

unas bolígrafos
*OO-nas
bol-EE-graf-os*
pens

unos lápices
OO-nos LA-pee-thes
pencils

un estuche
oon es-TOO-cheh
a pencil case

una goma
OO-na GO-ma
an eraser

un cuaderno
oon qua-DAIR-no
an exercise book

un pen drive
oon pen drive
a memory stick

un diccionario
oon dic-thee-o-NAR-ee-o
a dictionary

una calculadora
OO-na cal-coo-la-DOR-a
a calculator

OUT AND ABOUT

Generalmente, cogemos el
bus para ir al centro.
*Hen-eh-RAL-men-teh, co-HEH-mos el
bus PA-ra ir al THEN-tro.*
We usually get the bus to go into town.

Dos billetes de ida para en
centro, por favor.
*Dos bil-YEH-tes deh EE-da PA-ra el
THEN-tro, por fa-BOR.*
Two singles to the town centre, please.

un avión
oon a-bee-ON
a plane

un barco
oon BAR-co
a boat/ferry

una moto
OO-na MO-to
a motorbike

un taxi
oon TAK-see
a taxi

un aeropuerto
oon a-eh-ro-PWAIR-to
an airport

un tren
oon tren
a train

un coche
oon CO-cheh
a car

un (auto)bus
oon (au-to) bus
a bus

una vespino
OO-na bes-PEE-no
a scooter

una parada de bus
*OO-na pa-RA-da
deh bus*
a bus stop

una estación
OO-na es-ta-thee-ON
a railway station

¿Me puede decir por donde se va a la estación, por favor?
Meh PWEH-deh deth-EER por DON-deh seh ba a la es-ta-thee-ON, por fa-BOR?
Can you tell me how to get to the station, please?

¿A qué hora sale el próximo tren para...?
A keh O-ra SA-leh el prox-SEE-mo tren PA-ra...?
What time is the next train to...?

¿De qué anden sale?
Deh keh an-DEN SA-leh?
Which platform is it?

Dobla a la derecha.
DOB-la a la de-RETCH-a.
Turn right.

Dobla a la izquierda
DOB-la a la eeth-key-AIR-da.
Turn left.

Sigue todo recto.
SEE-geh TO-do REC-to.
Go straight on.

en la glorieta
en la glo-ree-EH-ta
at the roundabout

¿Por dónde se va a la playa?
Por DON-deh seh ba a la PLY-ya?
How do I get to the beach?

Toma el 23.
TO-ma el bain-tee-TRES.
Take bus 23.

en el cruce
en el CROO-theh
at the crossroads

en los semáforos
en los se-MA-fo-ros
at the traffic lights

en el puente
en el PWEN-teh
at the bridge

JUST THE JOB

Quiero ser médico.
Key-AIR-oh sair MEH-dee-co.
I'd like to be a doctor.

un ♂/una ♀ deportista
oon/OO-na deh-por-TEES-ta
a sportsperson

un ♂/una ♀ dentista
oon/OO-na den-TEES-ta
a dentist

un veterinario ♂/una
veterinaria ♀
*oon ve-tair-rin-A-ree-oh/
OO-na ve-tair-rin-A-ree-a*
a vet

un ♂/una ♀ periodista
oon/OO-na pair-ee-o-DEES-ta
a journalist

Cuando termine mis estudios
de secundaria, quiero trabajar
en una tienda.
*QUAN-do tair-MEE-neh mees es-TOO-
dee-os day se-kun-DA-ree-a, kee-AIR-ro
tra-ba-HAR en OO-na tee-EN-da.*
When I leave school, I want to
work in a shop.

una oficina
OO-na o-fi-THEE-na
an office

al aire libre
al AY-ray LEE-breh
outdoors

una fábrica
OO-na FAB-ri-ca
a factory

un cocinero ♂/una cocinera♀
oon co-thee-NAIR-ro/
OO-na co-thee-NAIR-ra
a chef

un mecánico ♂/
una mujer mecánico ♀
oon me-KA-nee-ko/
OO-na mu-HAIR me-KA-nee-ko
a mechanic

un fotógrafo ♂/una
fotógrafa ♀
oon fo-TO-gra-fo/
OO-na fo-TO-gra-fa
a photographer

un bombero ♂/una
mujer bombero♀
oon bom-BAIR-ro/una mu-HAIR
bom-BAIR-ro
a firefighter

un ♂científico/una ♀ científica
oon thee-en-TEE-fi-ko/
OO-na thee-en-TEE-fi-ka
a scientist

un ♂/una ♀ policía
oon/OO-na po-lee-THEE-a
a police officer

Tengo un trabajo a tiempo parcial.
TEN-go oon tra-BA-ho a
tee-EM-po par-thee-AL.
I have a part-time job.

hacer de canguro
a-THAIR deh kan-GU-ro
babysitting

Reparto periódicos por la
mañana.
Re-PAR-toh pe-ree-OH-di-cos
por la man-YA-na.
I deliver newspapers
in the morning.

pasear a los perros
pass-eh-AR a los PAIR-ross
walking dogs

cortar el césped
cor-TAR el THES-ped
mowing the lawn

FEELING GOOD?

¿Qué tal?
Keh tal?
How are you?

Regular.
Reh-goo-LAR.
Not so great.

Muy bien, gracias.
Mwee bee-EN,
GRA-thee-as.
I'm fine, thanks.

Estoy contento ♂/
contenta ♀
Es-TOY con-TEN-to/con-TEN-ta.
I'm happy.

Estoy triste.
Estoy TREE-steh.
I'm sad.

Tengo miedo.
TEN-go mee-EH-do.
I'm scared.

Estoy un poco aburrido.
Es-TOY oon PO-co
a-boo-REE-do.
I'm a bit bored.

Lo estoy pasando
bien aquí.
Lo es-TOY pa-SAND-oh
bee-EN a-KEE.
I'm having fun here.

Estoy enfadado/
enfadada.
Es-TOY en-fa-DA-do/
en-fa-DA-da.
I'm angry.

¿Qué piensas?
Keh pee-EN-sas?
What do you think?

genial
heh-nee-AL
great

¡Es guay!
Es goo-AY!
It's really cool!

fácil
FA-theel
easy

divertido
dee-ber-TEE-tho
fun

difícil
di-FEE-theel
difficult

interesante
in-tair-res-SAN-teh
interesting

un desastre
oon de-SAS-treh
rubbish

¿Te sientes mal?
Teh see-EN-tes mal?
Not feeling well?

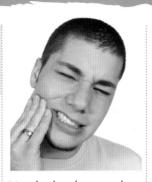

Me duelen las muelas.
Meh DWEL-en las MWEL-as.
I have toothache.

Tengo hambre.
TEN-go AM-breh.
I'm hungry.

Tengo sed.
TEN-go seth.
I'm thirsty.

Tengo ganas de vomitar.
TEN-go GA-nas deh bo-mee-TAR.
I feel sick.

Tengo frío.
TEN-go FREE-o.
I'm cold.

Tengo fiebre.
TEN-go fee-EH-bray.
I've got a temperature.

Quisiera ver un médico.
Key-see-AIR-a bair oon MEH-dee-co.
I'd like to see a doctor.

Tengo calor.
TEN-go ca-LOR.
I'm hot.

Estoy cansado ♂
/cansada ♀
*Es-TOY can-SA-do/
can-SA-da.*
I'm tired.

Tengo sueño.
TEN-go SWEN-yo.
I feel sleepy.

Me duele el estómago.
Meh DWEL-eh el es-TOM-a-go.
I've got a stomach ache.

Me duele la cabeza.
Meh DWEL-eh la ca-BEH-tha.
I've got a headache.

PRONUNCIATION GUIDE

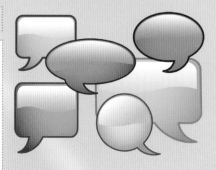

LIBRARY &
INFORMATION SERVICES

Spanish	How to make this sound
a	'a' as in 'cat'
e	'e' as in 'egg'
i	'i' as in 'it'
o	'o' as in 'hot'
u	'oo' as in 'food'
y	'ee' as in 'see' when it means 'and', but when it comes at the end of a word it sounds more like the 'y' in toy
ai/ay	'i' as in 'five'
au	'ou' as in 'found'
ei	'ey' as in 'they'
oi, oy	'oy' as in 'toy'
c (before a, o, u,)	'c' as in 'cat'
c (before e, i)	'th' as in 'think'
qu	'k' as in 'kitten'
g (before a, o, ue)	'g' as in 'gas'
g (before e, i)	'he' or 'hi' as in 'help' and 'his'
h	In Spanish, this letter is silent.
j	'h' as in 'hat'
ll	'll' as in 'million'
ñ	'ni' as in 'onion'
v	'b' as in 'bubble'
z	'th' as in 'thin'
r	roll this sound on the tip of your tongue

b, d, f, l, m, n, p, s, t, ch	as in English

STRESS IN SPANISH

If a Spanish word ends with an a consonant (apart from 's'), the final syllable is usually stressed.

In words ending with a vowel or 's', the stress usually falls on the second-to-last syllable.

* In Spanish you can make a statement into a question by making your voice go up at the end:

Statement: Es bueno.
Es boo-en-oh.
It's good.

Question: ¿Es bueno?
Es boo-en-oh?
Is it good?